Practice series : 5
Attachment and separation

About the author

Dr Vera Fahlberg, a psychotherapist with a paediatric background, is Medical Director of Forest Heights Lodge, Colorado, USA, a psychiatric treatment centre for emotionally disturbed boys. She is consultant to various Departments of Social Services and is often called on to provide expert testimony in court cases involving children.

First published by
Michigan Department of Social Services 1979

Published by
British Agencies for Adoption & Fostering
August 1981
Second impression April 1982
Reprinted February 1985
Copyright © Vera Fahlberg

ISBN 0 903534 37 1
ISSN 0260 - 0803

Acknowledgment

BAAF is grateful to Dr Vera Fahlberg for permission to publish thre workbooks which she and her colleagues developed from the *Trainir of children in foster care* project co-sponsored by the Michigan Department of Social Services, Spaulding for Children of Michigan a Forest Heights Lodge, Evergreen, Colorado, with a grant from the E McConnell Clark Foundation.

The workbooks, *Attachment and separation, Helping children when they must move* and *Child development* were formulated, refined, a validated over a period of three years by 33 agencies involved in the training project.

Dr Fahlberg readily gave us permission to make minor changes to th text to make it applicable to the British scene. This has involved changes in spelling and some descriptions of procedures and facilitie In no way, however, has the core of the work been changed.

Contents

Fantasy   4

About this Workbook   5

Section 1   **Introduction**   7
Attachment is defined and the long-range importance of a healthy attachment between parent and child is outlined. The proper role of the child care system in serving children and families with attachment problems is described.

Section 2   **Development of attachment between parent and child**   11
The way attachment comes about in normal parent-child relationships is described here.

Section 3   **Assessing attachment**   20
A set of checklists that help identify what to look at when assessing attachment are included.

Section 4   **Separation**   29
In the initial part of this section children's reactions to separation are described. Techniques that help children minimise the trauma of moves from one family to another are discussed in the second part.

Section 5   **Identifying and overcoming attachment problems**   38
In this section signs and symptoms of lack of attachment in children are identified and ways to heighten attachment are suggested.

Fantasy

Imagine yourself in a situation like this . . .

You and your spouse are at the dinner table. You are in the midst of a heated argument that has been going on for some time.

Suddenly there is a knock at the door. A stranger walks i looks as you and says 'You must come with me'.

Imagine that your spouse does nothing.
How do you feel?

Imagine that your spouse cries and clings to you, saying 'Don't go . . . Don't let them take you'.
How do you feel?

Imagine that your spouse says 'Go ahead. Good riddance'.
How do you feel?

Imagine that your spouse fights for you.
How do you feel?

This is a fantasy about being separated from the person to whom you are attached. Many foster children have lived through separation experiences like these. This workbook is about attachment and separation.

About this workbook

Every child who comes into care is in crisis. These children have been removed from the homes of their parents, often unexpectedly and abruptly. If these children have a bond or an attachment to their parents, they are in crisis because of this separation. Some of these abused or neglected children may have no attachment to their parents or may have attachments that are extremely problematic. This means it is likely that they have serious developmental problems.

Attachment between humans is a complex matter. The way attachments develop and function is not yet completely understood. However, we believe it is essential that professionals who serve children and families and participate in major decisions about their lives understand as much as possible about attachment. Helping children and families handle problems with attachment and separation is at the heart of child care.

In this workbook, we attempt to present material about attachment and separation in a way that is useful to people in the field. We attempt to tie theoretical material to the practical questions asked by social workers, mental health practitioners, school personnel, and others.

We have had extensive experiences in presenting this material to child care staff. They have taught us that it is easy to feel overwhelmed by the content and immobilised by guilt about past mistakes. It is our hope that the reader will use this material to think about new ways of dealing with children currently on a caseload rather than focusing on the past.

We hope that upon a first reading you will be able to identify a new technique or idea to use with a child who is handling an attachment and/or separation issue. In addition, we hope it will also stand as a reference to which one can return when faced with problems.

This workbook has five major sections. The first defines attachment and explores its relevance in child care. Section 2, 'The development of attachment between parent and child' describes the normal way that bonding occurs. This information serves as a base for the practical material in the rest of the workbook.

Section 3 offers checklists for 'Assessing attachment'. 'Separation' is the topic of Section 4. In this section, we discuss things that influence a child's reaction to separation and ways to help a child handle a move from one family to another. Finally Section 5 is entitled 'Identifying and overcoming attachment problems'. In it we review signs and symptoms of faulty attachment in children and suggest ways to enhance bonding.

Exercises have been interspersed throughout the text. They ask the reader to apply the material to practice. We think these exercises can be

useful to the individual who wishes to use this material as a workboo
We also have found that the exercises may be used in a staff meeting
with groups of foster parents or serve as a basis for training worksho
on this material.

Introduction

What is attachment?

Attachment has been defined as 'an affectionate bond between two individuals that endures through space and time and serves to join them emotionally' (Kennell, 1976). When a child has a strong and healthy bond to his parent, it allows him to develop both trust in others and reliance on himself. The bond that a child develops to the person who cares for him in his early years is the foundation of his future psychological, physical, and cognitive development and for his future relationships with others. Below we highlight the many positive effects of a child's strong attachment to his parent. Many children who come into care are in jeopardy of losing all these strengths. Selma Fraiberg has noted that children who do not have an attachment 'have been deprived of their humanity' (Fraiberg, 1977).

Attachment helps the child:
- *attain his full intellectual potential;*
- *sort out what he perceives;*
- *think logically;*
- *develop a conscience;*
- *become self-reliant;*
- *cope with stress and frustration;*
- *handle fear and worry;*
- *develop future relationships;*
- *reduce jealousy.*

Attachment in abused and neglected children

A basic psychological task faced by every individual is to find a comfortable and healthy balance between autonomy or self reliance, and dependency or trust in others. No one achieves this balance once and for all. It is, instead, shifted and renegotiated throughout life. The balance between autonomy and dependency is affected by major events such as marriage, the birth of a child, or the death of a loved one. The kinds of needs each of us has for dependency and autonomy and the way we achieve a balance between them seems to be strongly influenced by the way we were parented.

Many parents who abuse and neglect their children seem to have an imbalance in needs for dependency and autonomy. Some abusive parents appear to have an excessive urge for autonomy and independence. They have difficulty asking for help or receiving it when it is offered. They don't seem able to trust others; they equate any form of dependency with loss of control. This excessive autonomy is frequently compensation for the fact that their early dependency needs were not met by their own parents.

On the other hand, some abusive and neglectful parents are very dependent on others to meet their needs. They cannot meet the needs of their own children, and many in fact require the child to help them. When the children are unable to meet the parents' unreasonable needs, the parents may become frustrated, angry, and abusive.

Most children who come into care have come from families in which the needs of the parents have made it difficult for the children to learn to achieve a healthy balance between needs for dependency and autonomy. Without other kinds of experiences, these foster children will eventually become parents who will have difficulty helping their own children with these issues. Thus, one of the objectives of foster care should be to recognise these imbalances in the needs of the children and to help foster parents create an environment that allows the child to form a healthy bond to a parent and go on to other developmental tasks.

Attachment and children in foster care

Foster care can help children develop a sense of trust and a sense of self-reliance. It can be an opportunity for children to have some experiences with parents that can improve the way they function and the way that they are able to relate to others. If this is to happen, however, children need to be helped to develop healthy attachments.

The social worker's first responsibility is to maintain the child in his family and to work to improve the child's attachment to his biological parents. If, however, the child must be removed from his birth family and placed in a foster family, the foster parents' roles ought to be two-fold: to help the child develop healthy attachments and to aid in transferring these attachments to the permanent caretakers of the child who may be either birth parents or adoptive parents.

In order to do this effectively, foster parents and foster children need to develop bonds. In the past, the growth of such attachments has often been discouraged. Those who discourage such bonds between foster parents and children are encouraging emotional neglect of the children involved.

This means that foster parents must be selected and trained who have the ability to form normal attachments. Social worker must develop their abilities to assess attachment in children, to identify attachment problems, and to help families develop and transfer attachments.

Attachment and permanent planning

In human societies the initial bonding occurs between the infant and his primary caretaker who is usually his mother figure. This primary care-taker may be a birth mother, foster mother, or adoptive mother. In some cases, the primary caretaker is the father. Neither blood ties to the child nor sex of the primary caretaker seem to be as important as the relationship this person has to the child. In most societies the infant and his mother are members of a larger unit, the family. This family provides an excellent context for attachments with the child to grow. The following highlights the functions the family plays in relation to children.

Things the family provides for children:
— *a primary caretaker for the child;*
— *care by specific adults to whom the child can become attached;*
— *continuous contact with these adults on a day-to-day basis;*
— *continuous but changing relationships with a small number of individuals over a lifetime;*
— *safety and security;*
— *stimulation and encouragement for growth;*
— *reasonable expectations;*
— *experience in identifying and expressing emotions;*
— *support in times of stress.*

Studies done of children raised in institutions have shown that adequate physical care is not enough to lead to the development of a physically and psychologically healthy child. A primary person to whom the child can become attached, who responds to the child's needs and who initiates positive activities with the child seems to be indispensable. Although this primary caretaker doesn't have to meet all the child's needs all the time, usually she is responsible for the child most of the time and makes arrangements for his care in her absence.

This kind of day-to-day care by a primary caretaker provided in a family context has traditionally been provided for children in foster care. However, there are other aspects of family care that foster children have been denied. Many children in foster care have moved from one family to another and have not experienced relationships to members of a family over a long period of time.

This continuous but constantly changing contact with a small number of individuals is important. The relationship between a parent and an infant changes when that child becomes a toddler. When the child is of school age his relationship to his parent changes once more. It is transformed again when the child becomes an adolescent, and when the adolescent leaves home.

Relationships continue to change when the children become parents of the next generation of the family. Many people upon reaching middle age find their parents have more and more dependency needs. In many cultures, the elderly become quite dependent on their children, thus completing a cycle.

It is this long-range relationship over time and space that truly defines attachment. The continually changing nature of such a lifetime bond helps individuals achieve a strong sense of identity and of responsibility. People who lack such long-term attachments may have more difficulty sorting out what to attribute to their own actions and what to attribute to changes in the environment.

Most families provide growing children with memories of their past and help them keep memories alive. This helps children develop a sense of self. In foster care, we often minimise the child's past. Sometimes, we also minimise the child's future as well. Often we do this because we are not sure what will happen in the future. This uncertainty may extend so far that we can't even tell the child who will be taking care of him next year. We focus only on the here and now.

We believe that all those involved in foster care need to do all that is possible to ensure that the child has a stable family to whom he can relate throughout his lifetime. If we do not do this we are neither meeting one of the child's most basic needs nor are we modelling the importance of foresight, planning, and responsibility for one's own actions.

In this introduction we have reviewed the relevance of attachment to child care. In order to deal with the attachment issues that are such a key to this work, one must understand how bonding normally occurs. In Section 2, we turn our attention to the way that attachment usually develops between parent and child.

Development of attachment between parent and child

Introduction

This section of the workbook describes the way attachment normally develops between parent and child. An understanding of this normal process must underlie much of what the social worker does with families and children.

Workers often find that they must assess the degree to which a child is attached to a family in order to make decisions about the case. An understanding of how child and parent behave when there is a normal attachment between them serves as a basis for such an assessment. Another important role workers need to play is to help a child develop a strong attachment to a parent. Sometimes this means helping to strengthen a faulty parent-child attachment; sometimes it means helping a child bond to a new foster or adoptive parent. Again, an understanding of the normal bonding process is critical.

In this section we discuss that normal process. First we look at the kinds of interactions that occur between parent and child and at the way these interactions change as the child develops. Then, we take a close look at how these parent-child interactions work to build attachment between them.

The attachment process and child development

Setting the stage for bonding

The stage is set for bonding between parents and child during the period between the child's conception and birth, called the pre-natal period. During this period, parents begin to develop images of what the unborn child will be like. They form expectations and hopes for their child, for themselves as parents, and for their relationship with their child.

Many conditions of the pre-natal period affect the kind of attachment that will develop between parent and child. Some of these factors include characteristics of the pregnancy itself such as the timing of the pregnancy, the mother's condition during the pregnancy, and the presence or absence of pre-natal complications.

In addition, the relationship between the child's parents during pregnancy affects the bonding that will occur with the child. The kind of parenting that the parents themselves received strongly influences the kinds of images that they will develop of their child and of themselves as parents. Characteristics of the infant *in utero* come into play as well. Mothers of more than one child by birth sometimes note marked differences in infants *in utero*; one may rarely move and another may kick and turn frequently. The characteristics of the child and the way the mother perceives them affect the bonds that will develop.

Adoptive parents can benefit from a period of 'psychological pregnancy'. During this time, they, too, can fantasise about what it will be like to be parents and imagine themselves acting as parents in a variety of situations. A very short pre-placement waiting period precludes this kind of preparation. On the other hand, waits of one to three years are too long and tend to erode the benefits of a psychological pregnancy.

Bonding at birth

Direct bonding between mother and child begins during the very first moments of the child's life. Desmond (1966) found that during the first hour of an infant's life he is wide awake and has his eyes wide open. After this, the infant falls into a deep sleep. Most mothers of newborns use their first contact with the child to explore him, to count fingers and toes, and just generally to see if he is physically normal.

When a newborn infant is held horizontally, he reflexively turns his head toward the person who is holding him. The mother is pleased when the infant looks at her. She tends to caress the child gently.

All of this exploring is part of the claiming process. During this process the mother is consciously and unconsciously looking for ways to tell her child from others. Studies based on videotapes of mother and child interactions made during deliveries and post-partum hospital stays indicate that when the mother doesn't take an active part in this claiming process the family is at high risk for severe parent-child difficulties in future years.

Bonding in the first six months

When an infant is born, his nervous system is complete, but it is not well organised. Especially during the first month of life, the newborn makes adjustments to life outside his mother's body. His perceptual threshold is high; that is, he is not sensitive to internal or external stimuli of which an older child would be clearly aware. The newborn is irregular in many areas; he doesn't eat, sleep, or eliminate on schedule. The infant startles when he perceives things, and he moves in a jerky, unco-ordinated way.

During the first year of life and thereafter, the child's nervous system will become better organised. The interactions between the newborn and his parents are a major force in this process. The influence of parent-child interactions on the child's developing nervous system may explain why children who are not well attached often have poor cognitive development.

The interactions between parent and child are exchanges between them that involve touch, sound, or visual stimulation. The child has capacities to participate in these exchanges even in the first six months of life. Children do not initially have control over their voluntary muscles. There is a natural order in which control over these muscles comes. In general, the child acquires muscle control from the head downward and from the central part of the body outward.

12

Therefore, it is with his face muscles that the infant begins to respond to the bonding process. The infant first learns to focus his eyes on objects eight or nine inches away. This is the distance between the infant's eyes and the mother's face when the child is nursing at the breast. Thus, when children are held at the breast, they first become capable of focusing on their mother's face. From the age of four weeks, infants prefer looking at the human face to looking at other kinds of stimuli. By eight or nine weeks the infant is able to follow the movement of the human face and attend to it closely.

Face-to-face contact is very important in developing bonds with an infant. Parents need to be aware of its importance. Spitz (1965) found that infants showed signs of pleasure even when they were presented with a mask of the human face. Covering up the lower part of the mask did not change their response. However, when the upper part of the mask was covered, even just one eye of it, the infants did not respond with pleasure. The infant's response to the human eyes seems to be innate rather than learned.

By the time they are three or three and a half months old, most infants begin to prefer looking at their mothers' faces to looking at other faces. Though infants at this age continue to show pleasure at other faces, responses of pleasure occur more strongly and consistently in response to the mother's face. This preference for a specific face develops a full two months before the infant shows pleasure at the sight of a bottle or other object.

From the time of birth, loud noises distress the infant and soft sounds quiet him. Wolff (1966) has demonstrated infants turn toward sounds and that from the time the child is three to four weeks old he recognises the voice of his mother. By age four weeks the infant gurgles and coos in response to the human voice. When mother or someone else responds to such vocalisations they increase. In fact, one of the functions of babbling seems to be to keep the mother close and to promote interaction between mother and child and thus to promote bonding.

Body contact between mother and child also contributes to bonding between them. In most societies children are in more frequent body contact with their mothers than they are in western industrialised countries. The rhythmic movements that the child experiences as he is carried about by his mother are similar to what he experienced before birth.

It has been found that experiencing rhythmic movement encourages growth among premature infants. Cradles and rocking chairs have long been used to help soothe fussy babies. In recent years an increasing number of mothers have been using a sling-like support called a Snugli to permit closeness with their babies as they go about their daily housework and go out on excursions. This closeness seems to be particularly soothing to fussy babies.

We have seen that even in these early months the infant responds most to the particular sensations that promote contact with others. They prefer looking at the human face and listening to the human voice.

13

They prefer the feel of soft clothes and the sense of rhythmical movements that they experience as their mother walks. They prefer the taste of their mother's milk. One might speculate that infants may prefer the smell of humans to other smells and may even be able to identify their primary caretaker through smell although we know of no studies in this area.

Thus, infants are especially sensitive to developing attachment behaviour during the fourth, fifth and sixth months of their lives. This is confirmed by studies such as those done by Yarrow in 1963. He found that 86 per cent of those infants in his study who were moved from a foster home to an adoptive home when they were six months old showed signs of disturbance. Every infant who was moved at the age of seven months or older showed marked disturbance.

Bonding from six months to twelve months

When he is between six and nine months old, the child can consistently distinguish between family members and strangers. By this age, the child begins to demonstrate fear or anxiety when he is approached by a stranger. The strength and frequency of these fear reactions increase as the child nears one year of age. This makes it increasingly difficult for a child to develop an attachment to a new primary caretaker during this period.

By the age of eight months, the child plays a more active part in trying to keep his mother close to him. The child obviously tries to catch the mother's attention. Since most children are somewhat mobile at this age, it becomes easier for them to achieve this aim. Such activities on the part of the child are a necessary part of forming an attachment, and should not be discouraged. By the age of one year, the child and mother will have developed a unique balance between them in terms of who initiates interactions, how they are initiated, and how they are responded to.

Often, we can virtually see this kind of delicate balance being achieved. The infant's urge for closeness and attachment is so strong that if his mother does not stay close to him, the child behaves in a way that tends to draw her to him. Such infants are often clingy and whiney. If the parent rejects the child at these times, the clinging and whiney behaviour increases. In these cases, closeness to mother is maintained with primarily negative rather than positive interactions.

If, however, the mother shows the child that she is ready to remain close to him, he can relax and free his energies for other activities. The nature of this balance between mother and child changes as the child develops. During the first year, attachment between mother and child should increase, but dependency should decrease. Attachment and dependency are not synonymous terms.

According to Ainsworth (1952) the anxious, the insecure child may falsely appear more strongly attached to his mother than the secure child who can explore fairly freely in a strange situation using his mother as a secure base; who is not distressed by the appearance of a stranger; and who shows awareness of his mother's absence, greets her on her return, and then resumes his previous activities.

In contrast, the insecure child is one who does not explore even when his mother is present; who becomes extremely alarmed by the appearance of a stranger; who seems helpless and in acute distress when his mother leaves, and on her return is either disinterested or in distress but in either case, incapable of making an organised attempt to reach her.

Bonding after one year

In general, one and two-year-old children continue to exhibit many kinds of attachment behaviour. The primary psychological task for a toddler is to recognise that he and his primary caretaker are two separate individuals. This is made easier because the toddler is increasingly able to get around by himself. He is able to perceive more and more of what is in his environment and is developing speech which helps increase his autonomy and his awareness of his own feelings and those of others. 'Me', 'mine', 'you', and 'no' are all words that help the two-year-old accomplish this task.

After the child is three, it becomes easier for him to accept his mother's temporary absence. However, throughout life attachment behaviour increases during times of anxiety and stress. Observing a child when he is tired, frightened, or not feeling well is often a useful way to find out about his attachment to his caretaker. The well-attached child will seek out his primary caretaker at this time and be comforted.

Even as adults, when we are sick, frightened, or vulnerable, we want to be close to the people to whom we are attached, and we may revert to dependent behaviour to keep them close.

Reciprocity between mother and child

We've seen that attachment between parent and child results from their interactions. These interactions begin at birth and continue and change as the child matures. We can analyse these interactions in terms of how they build the bond between mother and child.

Most of the interactions between a mother and her newborn child are initiated by the infant who fusses and cries when he is uncomfortable. The mother responds to these overtures. As the child gets older, an increasing percentage of interactions are initiated by the mother, and the child responds.

It is usual for many of the interactions between mother and child to be cyclical. In such cases the responses of one partner encourage the other to continue to respond. For example, the child cries because he is wet and uncomfortable; his mother responds by changing him and at the same time she talks and smiles at him; he smiles and gurgles back. The interaction is pleasurable for both and is likely to continue through a series of activities.

Bowlby (1970) says that there are two characteristics of the interactions between mother and child that strongly affect the kind and degree of attachment that will develop between them. These are the speed and intensity with which the mother responds to the infant's crying and the extent to which the mother initiates interactions with the infant. We will take a closer look at both interactions initiated by the child and those that the mother initiates and the way they contribute to attachment.

The arousal-relaxation cycle: its importance in bonding

We have noted that infants have a relatively high perceptual threshold. When, however, an infant experiences displeasure or tension, because of either internal or external stimuli, he discharges it. The infant moves his arms and legs; he becomes red in the face; he cries; he squirms. It is clear to everyone that he is uncomfortable.

As long as the infant is discharging this tension, his perception of the outside world is blocked. Thus, if an infant or child continually experiences tension, his ability to perceive what is going on around him is seriously limited. As a result, his intellectual development that depends on such perceptions is hampered or blocked.

The opposite of displeasure in an infant is not happiness or pleasure but is instead a state of quiescence or contentment. The parent's role when the infant is discharging this tension is to return the child to a quiescent state.

The following diagram depicts a typical, successful interaction between mother and child. The interaction is initiated by the child's need and consequent expression of displeasure and completed by the mother's response.

The arousal-relaxation cycle

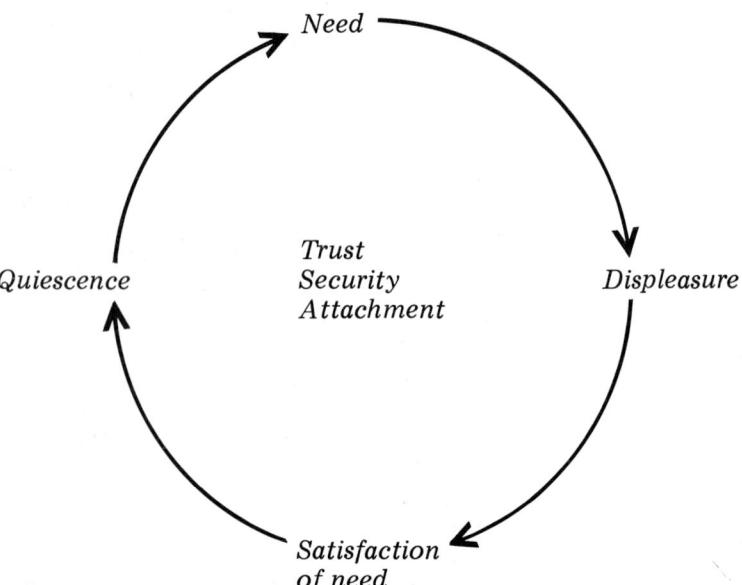

This cycle is what is called the 'arousal-relaxation cycle'. The repeated successful completion of this cycle is critical if the child is to develop a sense of trust and security and become attached to his mother.

Scrutiny of the diagram reveals several places where the successful completion of the arousal-relaxation cycle might break down for a mother and child pair. There is a tendency in our society today to blame parents, particularly the mothers, for any disturbance in their child's emotional development. It is true that some neglectful or abusive parents may fail consistently to respond to their children's overtures in a way that meets the child's needs and therefore disrupt this cycle of interactions.

This kind of parental lack of response is not, however, the only cause of disruption in the arousal-relaxation cycle. If for some reason the child does not experience states of discomfort, the cycle will not even be initiated. Parents of other children may try to respond to their infants but find themselves unable to relieve their discomfort. If a parent consistently meets the child's needs before he is uncomfortable or protects the child from any stimuli that would disturb him, the cycle is disrupted. Spitz (1965) states that it is probably as harmful to deprive an infant of the feeling of discomfort as to deprive him of the feeling of pleasure.

Many premature infants are examples of children whose behaviour may not readily fit into a pattern that promotes attachment between mother and child. These children generally do not respond to environmental stimuli in the same way as other infants. Their perceptual thresholds are so high that they are not aware of internal discomfort; in fact, they may have to be tube-fed on a regular schedule because they do not experience the same sensation of displeasure due to hunger. In addition, such infants are frequently isolated from other interactions such as being physically close to their mothers that lead to bonding.

Delacato (1974) has speculated that children with certain organic problems may have abnormal perceptual thresholds; higher than normal in some cases or lower than normal in others. This means that these children may either rarely experience discomfort or experience it very frequently. In either case the child would not regularly experience the relief from an unpleasant state that is key to forming an attachment to the mother. This theory may explain some cases of poor attachment between mother and child when mothering seems adequate.

A case example of a breakdown in the formation of attachment between mother and child that stemmed from an abnormality in the child follows.

I was asked to see a three-year-old boy who had delayed speech develop-ment and signs of lack of trust for his parents. The history revealed that this had been a planned pregnancy. The parents were hoping that this first child would be a boy; the marital situation was stable; and both parents seemed to be well-adjusted adults who had had their needs met as children.

However, the history also revealed that this child had developed seizures on the third day of life. They were a rather rare type with a poor prognosis. The parents were told that about one-third of the children with such seizures die within their first year; one-third are retarded, and the remainder are normal.

The child was put on medication. The mother was advised that the prognosis for this particular child could be somewhat anticipated by the effectiveness of the medication in controlling the seizures. The mother noted that if she touched him a lot, he tended to have a seizure. Being a 'good' mother, her reaction was obviously to minimise the amount she stimulated him. Although she met his basic physical needs, she did not hold him, rock him, or play with him during the first few months of his life.

His seizures ceased when he was six months old, but the child's disability had undermined his mother's confidence in her abilities to mother him. She undoubtedly continued to be somewhat restrained with him for fear she would reactivate the seizures.

We set up a programme that encouraged bonding between this three-year-old child and his parents. Despite a successful programme, some delays in the child's speech development remained. It will never be certain whether these delays resulted from brain damage that was related to the seizures or from the lack of stimulation he experienced in his first few months of life.

Initiation of positive interactions: its importance in bonding

We have seen that the arousal-relaxation cycle is initiated by the child's needs and that successful completion of this cycle contributes to bonding between mother and child. However, the extent to which the mother initiates interactions with the infant also influences the attachment between them. The diagram below illustrates the cycle of positive parent-child interaction that is initiated by the parent.

The positive interaction cycle

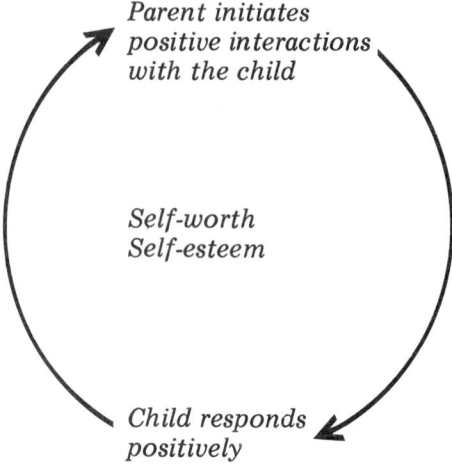

Parent initiates positive interactions with the child

Self-worth
Self-esteem

Child responds positively

There is some evidence that these sorts of social interactions between mother and child contribute more to the bonds between them than do the kind of interactions that occur around meeting the child's physical needs. For example, Ainsworth (1952) feels that social interactions, not routine care, are the most important part of mothering. The more social interactions an infant has with someone, the more strongly attached he becomes to that person.

In addition, it seems that a child who is well-attached to one person can more easily become attached to others. The fact that a child's strong attachment to one person eases the development of attachments to others is a critical one for foster care. It means that children can be helped to become attached to a foster parent, and then to extend that attachment to natural family members, adoptive parents, or others.

Section 3: **Assessing attachment**

As we try to assess attachment in various families we need to train ourselves to look at the child, the parents, and the environment. When we look at the child, we need to observe his developmental functioning. We also need to look at the behaviour he exhibits, particularly in his home. As we observe in the home, we look at his interactions with adults in general and parents in particular and his interactions with siblings and peers.

Observing parents includes how they react to the child's overtures; the interactions that they initiate with the child; disciplinary techniques used in the home; and the parents' awareness of the child as a separate individual who has needs of his own rather than relating all of the child's behaviour to their needs. In addition, we need to know if the environment provides both adequate stimulation and safety measures appropriate to the child's age and stage of development.

The four Observation Checklists that follow include some specific items to note in order to assess the child's attachment level. You may wish to add others in the blank spaces. In all cases, looking at the environment should be included with your observations of child and parents.

Observation checklist:
What to look for in assessing attachment

1: Birth to one year

Does the child . . . ?	Does the parent(s) . . . ?

- *appear alert?*
- *respond to humans?*
- *show interest in the human face?*
- *track with his eyes?*
- *vocalise frequently?*
- *exhibit expected motor development?*
- *enjoy close physical contact?*
- *exhibit discomfort?*
- *appear to be easily comforted?*
- *exhibit normal or excessive fussiness?*
- *appear outgoing or is he passive and withdrawn?*
- *have good muscle tone?*
  others:
	- *respond to the infant's vocalisations?*
	- *change voice tone when talking to the infant or about the infant?*
	- *show interest in face to face contact with the infant?*
	- *exhibit interest in and encourage age appropriate development?*
	- *respond to the child's indications of discomfort?*
	- *show the ability to comfort the child?*
	- *enjoy close physical contact with the child?*
	- *initiate positive interactions with the child?*
	- *identify positive or negative qualities in the child that remind the parent of another family member?*
	  others:

Observation checklist:

What to look for in assessing attachment

2: One to five years

Does the child . . . ?	Does the parent(s) . . . ?
- explore the environment in a normal way? *- respond to parent(s)?* *- keep himself occupied in a positive way?* *- seem relaxed and happy?* *- have the ability to express emotions?* *- react to pain and pleasure?* *- engage in age appropriate activity?* *- use speech appropriately?* *- express frustration?* *- respond to parental limit setting?* *- exhibit observable fears?* *- react positively to physical closeness?* *- respond appropriately to separation from parent?* *- respond appropriately to parent's return?* *- exhibit body rigidity or relaxation?* *others:*	*- use appropriate disciplinary measures?* *- show interest in child's development?* *- respond to child's overtures?* *- encourage physical closeness with the child?* *- comfort the child in a positive way?* *- initiate positive interactions with the child?* *- accept expressions of autonomy?* *- see the child as 'taking after' someone? Is this positive or negative?* *others:*

3: *Primary school children*

Does the child . . . ?	Does the parent(s) . . . ?
- behave as though he likes himself? *- appear proud of accomplishments?* *- share?* *- perform well academically?* *- always test limits?* *- try new tasks?* *- react realistically to making a mistake? Does he show fear, anger, or acceptance?* *- have the ability to express emotions?* *- establish eye contact?* *- exhibit confidence in his abilities or does he frequently say 'I don't know'?* *- appear to be developing a conscience?* *- move in relaxed way or is there body rigidity?* *- feel comfortable speaking to adults?* *- smile easily?* *- react to parent(s) being physically close?* *- have positive interactions with siblings and/or peers?* *- appear comfortable with his sexual identification?* *others:*	*- show interest in child's school performance?* *- accept expression of negative feelings?* *- respond to child's overtures?* *- give support for child in terms of developing healthy peer relationships?* *- handle problems between siblings equitably?* *- initiate affectionate overtures?* *- use appropriate disciplinary measures?* *- assign age appropriate responsibilities to the child?* *others:*

4: Adolescents

Is the adolescent . . . ?	Does the parent(s) . . . ?
- *aware of his strong points?* - *aware of his weak points?* - *comfortable with his sexuality?* - *engaging in positive peer interactions?* - *performing satisfactorily in school?* - *exhibiting signs of conscience development?* - *free from severe problems with the law?* - *accepting and/or rejecting parents' value system?* - *keeping himself occupied in appropriate ways?* - *comfortable with reasonable limits or is he constantly involved in control issues?* - *developing interests outside the home?* *others:*	- *set appropriate limits?* - *encourage appropriate autonomy?* - *trust the adolescent?* - *show interest in and acceptance of adolescent's friends?* - *display interest in adolescent's school performance?* - *exhibit interest in adolescent's outside activities?* - *have reasonable expectations of chores and/or responsibilities adolescent should assume?* - *stand by the adolescent if he gets into trouble?* - *show affection?* - *think this child will 'turn out' okay?* *others:*

Exercise 1:
Identifying signs of attachment — instructions

Purpose:
To help you learn what types of comments and/or observations in case records aid in assessing a child's attachment.

How to do it:
1 *Read Danny's case history on the next page.*

2 *Look at the* Observation checklist 2: What to look for in assessing attachment — one to five years *on page 22*

3 *Make a worksheet like that on page 28 and list comments and/or observations from the case record that you feel will aid in assessing Danny's attachment to each of his parents. Consider his attachment to each parent individually.*

4 *After working on your list, look at page 28 where a sample analysis of the case appears and compare your worksheet with the sample.*

Danny, age two and a half, the son of Carl and Tammy T. was born premature and with a cleft palate. He had a history of failure to thrive during infancy. He was hospitalised repeatedly for this condition, and in the hospital he always gained weight. At six months he 'accidentally' broke his leg while his father was overseas. At present, Danny has been in foster care for several months. Reportedly, Carl abused Danny leading to a black eye and bruises on the buttocks. It was Tammy who called the caseworker and reported the abuse, knowing her report probably would lead to admission to care.

The parents have not followed through with therapy as ordered by the court. They recently separated and are planning a divorce. The father in particular has asked for Danny's custody.

In her interview, Tammy reported that Danny is in care 'because my husband got mad and hit him'. She does not see Danny as a child who easily frustrates adults although she stated that she gets frustrated when 'he deliberately wets his pants'. She sees Danny as closely resembling his father. Tammy was unable to give any information about what Danny liked to play or how he kept himself occupied when he was at home. She stated that he is affectionate and 'easy going now'.

When the father was interviewed, he readily admitted spanking Danny excessively with a belt, but stated that the black eye occurred when Danny ran from him to avoid a spanking, slipped, and hit his eye on the corner of the bed. The discipline was taking place because Danny had repeatedly got out of bed when put down for a nap. Tammy was napping at the time according to Carl and did not see what happened. Carl is able to give considerable information about Danny's likes and dislikes. He, too, sees Danny as resembling himself.

Tammy initially refused to visit with Danny in the nursery at the time of the evaluation because 'he is not interested in seeing me; he is more interested in the toys'. Carl played with Danny in the nursery while Tammy was being interviewed. Danny did not protest when his father left the nursery to go with the interviewer. The father reassured Danny that he would be back shortly and made a point of leaving his coat in the nursery as he told Danny that he would be back.

When we tried to test Danny, he protested about the separation and asked his father to go with him. On the way to the office, Danny imitated his father's walk with thumbs in pocket. He crawled up into his father's lap in the office, took off his dad's glasses, and put them on. His dad's comment as he took his glasses back was 'Oh, you remember our little game'. Carl was interested and pleased with Danny's performance levels during the testing. Although we had some difficulty understanding Danny's speech, Carl did not.

When Tammy came in mid-way during the testing, Danny interrupted his task and ran to her with arms up-raised. She picked him up, and her affect was appropriate. When his parents left, Danny indicated that he did not want them to. He clung to his mother and clearly said 'I want to go with you'. He cried momentarily and tried to follow when they left, but he was easily distracted following their departure.

Exercise 1:
Identifying signs of attachment — worksheet

Danny and mother	Danny and father
1. Danny ran to mother	1. Father knows Danny's likes and dislikes
2. Mother picked up Danny and showed affection	2. Carl played with Danny in the nursery
3. Danny did not want his mother to leave	3. Carl left coat in nursery to reassure Danny that he would return
4.	4. Danny protested separation from father
5.	5. Danny imitated father's walk
6.	6. Danny crawled on his father's lap
7.	7. Carl understood Danny's speech

Section 4: **Separation**

Imagine yourself in a situation like this . . .

You are at home at night. You have put your three children
to bed and have just gone to bed yourself. Your spouse is out
for the evening and won't be home until later. Everything is
quiet, and you are settling down to sleep . . .

Suddenly there is a knock on the door, quickly followed
by heavy footsteps. Someone in uniform enters your bedroom
and announces, 'You're coming with me'. He takes you and
your children outside.

You all get into a car. You drive into a strange neighbourhood, far from your home. The car stops in front of a house.
You are left in the car as one of the children is taken to the
door of the house. The man in uniform knocks; someone
answers the door; and your child is handed over to this
person. The uniformed man returns to the car.

You drive further. The man takes your second child and
leaves him at another strange house.

He drives further. He stops. You and your third child are
taken to the door of a house. He knocks and when a person
answers, the uniformed man says, 'Here they are'. You are
handed over to the person in this house and left there.

— *How did you feel when the person came into the house?*
— *How did you feel when you left your neighbourhood?*
— *How did you feel as you were separated from your children?*
— *How did you feel as you were handed over to a stranger?*
— *What would you want to do?*

A child coming into foster care may experience similar
feelings.

Introduction

Most children who enter care, or move from one foster home to another,
or move into an adoptive home experience separation from the person
or persons to whom they are attached. One of the serious challenges in
child care is helping children handle these traumatic separations.

In this section we first discuss children's reactions to separation and
the things that affect those reactions. We then suggest ways that both
workers and foster parents can help children deal with the separations
that occur when they move from one family to another.

Reactions to separation

Children differ in the way they respond to being separated from their parents. This response varies from severe depression in children who are well-attached to their parents and then abruptly separated from them to almost no reaction in children who have been emotionally neglected and have virtually no attachment to their parents. The reactions of most children who come into care fall between those two extremes.

The child's reaction to separation from his parent can provide the worker with valuable information about the attachment between them. There are several important influences on the child's reaction to separation. These include:

— *the nature of the child's attachment to his primary caretakers;*
— *the nature of the primary caretaker's bonding to the child;*
— *the experiences the child has had with separation in the past;*
— *his perceptions of the reasons for the separation;*

does the child view the separation as his fault? Children whose parents have been hostile or irritable and have threatened the child with separation seem to be particularly affected by it.

— *the circumstances of the move itself; and*

whether the child has been prepared for the move or not, the attitudes of the people around him and his ability to express his feelings and have them accepted all influence the child's reaction to separation.

— *the environment from which he is being moved;*

despite shortcomings that others may see in the child's environment, from the child's viewpoint the known is nearly always better than the unknown. However, if a child is actually fearful of his living environment, he may not react to the separation so much.

All these factors influence a child's reaction to separation. In helping a child handle a separation, it is useful to know what a 'normal' reaction to separation is.

Bowlby (1970) describes three stages that well-attached children go through when they are separated from the person to whom they are attached. These stages are most evident in the young child. They are:

1 the child protests vigorously and makes attempts to recover his mother, such as going to the door and trying to find her;

2 the child despairs of recovering his mother, but he continues to be watchful. He appears to be preoccupied constantly and depressed. When a car drives up or when there is a noise at the door, he becomes alert, hoping that his mother is returning; and

3   the child becomes emotionally detached and appears to lose interest in mothers.

What follows is a case example of a child who was well attached and then separated.

Case example
At the time we saw John, he was four and had been in foster care for about three months. During his first six weeks in care, he was placed in an emergency foster home. During his stay in this home John was fussy and cried constantly.

In his second foster placement he was not so much fussy as withdrawn. He played for hours by himself, talking to himself in baby voices and making peculiar sounds. He had good eye contact with us when we examined him, but he seemed indiscriminately affectionate; he seemed to respond equally warmly to all adults. He was at his age level on developmental tests and was in good contact with reality.

The history revealed that John had lost his mother when he was 18 months old. His father became his primary caretaker. While he was moving and getting settled, he left John with an aunt. John had had almost no contact with the aunt before he was left there.

With the aunt he became very fussy. He regressed in toileting and smeared faeces. He alternated between being very depressed and having temper tantrums. The aunt had placed John in foster care.

When John was in the second foster placement, his father came for his first visit with the child. John's face 'lit up' when he first saw his father. He then looked apprehensive and acted ambivalent about getting close to his father. His father initiated many positive interactions with John. Eventually, John was able to say 'Don't ever leave me again, Daddy'.

John's history illustrates the stages that Bowlby describes as common in well-attached children who are separated. Because a history of strong attachment is rare in child care or because workers fail to recognise this sort of behaviour for what it is, there is a danger that children who have this kind of reaction may be classified as 'severely disturbed'.

It is not unusual for a child to act aggressively during separations from his parents and be very ambivalent toward them when he visits them or returns home. The child does not plan to act this way but does so in response to unconscious stimuli. The function of this behaviour is to assist in the reunion process and to discourage his parents from leaving him again. Hence, this behaviour promotes rather than discourages bonding.

When this kind of behaviour occurs during visits between parent and child, all involved may tend to say that the visits are upsetting the child and should be stopped. Similarly, if this kind of behaviour occurs when the child is returned home to his parents, workers sometimes misinterpret the behaviour and assume the parents are doing something wrong. The parents may feel that way too. Actually, the child's negative behaviour stems from a healthy need. When a child returns home from foster care, workers need to make special efforts to support the parents and help them handle the child's anger over the past separation.

Reactions to threatened separation

Social workers also need to understand the relationship between fear and attachment. The primary function of attachment behaviour in the animal kingdom is protection from the aggression of predators. In human families, too, attachment behaviour is heightened when a family member is threatened. The function of both fear and attachment is protection. Sometimes the social worker who is considering removing a child from a family embodies a threat.

In such a situation, the child may cling to the parent and exhibit hostility or fear of the worker. This reaction is characterised by withdrawal from the feared object and movement toward a trusted person.

Sometimes there is conflict between the two aspects of this reaction. The diagrams below illustrate such a dilemma. Both diagrams portray a child, a dog, and a parent. In both cases the child wants to get away from the dog and get close to his parents.

Figure 1

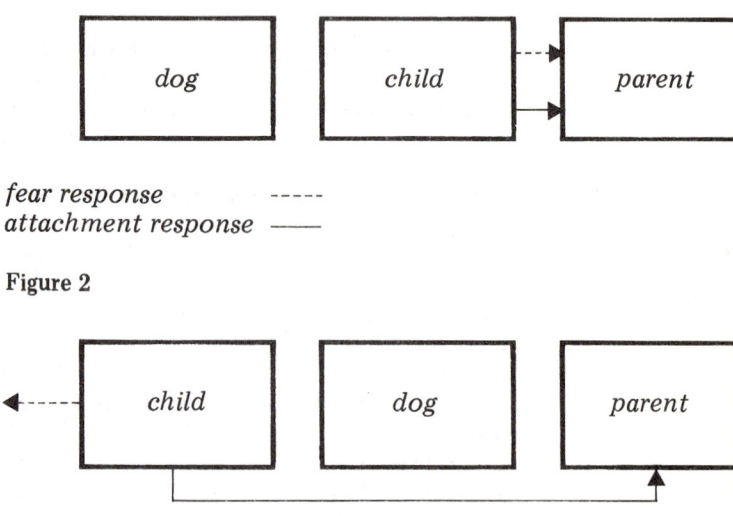

fear response - - - - -
attachment response ——

Figure 2

In figure 1, the child can get away from the dog and also get close to his parent. In figure 2, however, the child faces a dilemma. If he moves further from the object he fears, he also moves further from the person to whom he is attached. Most attached children, up to an age where they can think well conceptually, will choose moving closer to the attachment object over withdrawing from the feared object.

Thus we can understand why an abused child may cling to his abusive parent when the social worker enters the home. Though the child may fear the parent, he may also be attached to her. He both fears the social worker and has no attachment to her. He chooses the parent.

The most frightening thing for a child is to be afraid and to be separated from his attachment object simultaneously. This is why moves are so frightening. All people's fears are more easily heightened when they are away from those to whom they are attached.

Making moves easier for a child: the worker's role

Most children's immediate reaction to an abrupt separation from their parents or to abandonment by them is intense anxiety. If the worker makes a comment like 'Most kids are really scared when they move into a new home', it frequently opens the door for the child to talk about his feelings.

This means that the social worker must deal with what happens when that door opens. It is important that workers be honest with children when they are moving from one home to another. They cannot gloss over the situation by telling the child that everything is going to be 'fine'. It also means that the worker may have to admit not knowing the answers to questions that the child asks.

If the child wants to know how long he will be in care and the placement is an emergency one, the worker may have to say that it will depend upon a court hearing the next day, or upon when the parents can be located, or whatever the truth is in each case. The child also needs to be assured that he will have frequent contact with the social worker early in the placement and will be informed about the plans made for his future.

The child then needs, first, permission to express his feelings and second, acceptance of the feelings, no matter what they are. Social workers must avoid the tendency to minimise the child's feelings. Simply saying 'Don't be sad' or 'It's not your fault!' is not helpful. The child's pain does not go away because the adults around him ignore it or are uncomfortable with it.

At the time of a move the child has very intense feelings, and he is in a state of high arousal. It is a time when someone who helps the child cope with his feelings can build trust with him. This situation can be used to help build an attachment between the child and the adults who can accept his feelings. This makes use of the arousal-relaxation cycle described in Section 2.

The positive use of a painful and frightening situation for the child can occur only if the adults involved take on the job of helping the child deal with his feelings. Many children who come into care have already learned that it is not safe to let adults know how they feel, and there is a danger that this learning will be reinforced as the child moves into foster care. The child who doesn't express strong feelings may be easier to deal with in the short run but in the long run he is likely to fare poorly. Expression of feelings can have therapeutic consequences for the child and lead to psychological growth; lack of such expression can lead to stagnation.

Most children who come into care are removed from their homes in an emergency situation. Usually the child has little advance warning and is not prepared to be separated from his family. After experiencing such a move, the child is likely to be more prone to suffering underlying anxiety about the unknowns in his future.

It is difficult to overcome the negative effects of this kind of traumatic initial separation. However, it is possible to use further moves or separations to teach the child that all moves do not lead to the same feelings or to the same outcome. Thus, the child should be prepared for a move whenever possible. Once the child is in care there are only very rare events, such as the death or emergency hospitalisation of a foster family member or abuse in the foster home, that justify moving a child without preparing him for that move.

Making moves easier for the child: the foster family's role

Foster parents should play an important role in helping to prepare a child to move when he leaves their home and in helping a child handle a move when he enters their home. Traditionally, foster parents have not been helped or supported in this process which is painful for them as well as for the child. We will delineate briefly a few important things foster parents can do to help a child move. A more complete discussion of ways to minimise the trauma of the various moves associated with foster care is in the workbook on moving in this series.

When the child leaves the foster home
We have said that when children move they experience very intense feelings. These feelings may range from fear, anger, uncertainty, help-lessness, or resignation to relief. Foster parents can help a child who leaves their family to express these feelings. Some foster parents need a method to help them do this. One technique that has worked has been for the social worker to show the child a list of feelings and help him to identify his particular feelings. The social worker can then share this information with the foster parents.

Foster parents can also think about their own feelings about the move because often their own feelings are similar to the child's. It is particularly important at the time of the move for the child to know that the foster family cared about him. Letting the child know that he was cared about is not placing a burden on him, but rather it teaches him that relationships are important.

When children leave a home they also need to understand why they are moving. They need to be talked to straight about that. This helps make it unnecessary for the child to do a lot of the testing in the new family that he would otherwise do.

When a child enters the home
When children move into a new foster family that family can use the

34

fact that the child is in great discomfort to build an attachment between themselves and the child. If they help the child express his feelings, they alleviate some of his discomfort and increase his attachment to them.

Children need permission to miss their former family. If not given this kind of permission, some children may misbehave so they will be spanked so that they can cry for the family they have left. It helps, too, if the child knows that his former family wishes that he do well in his new home and hears that they are pleased when he does.

When a child is removed from his birth family, the most appropriate thing the foster family can do is to comfort the child physically, talk little, and accept the feelings from loss to anger that the child may have.

Fears, anxieties, nightmares, or night terrors are very common for children who are separated from their parents. Some children will withdraw more and will not want to talk. In these cases, foster parents can be physically close without insisting on talking. When a child is angry, foster parents can accept the anger and at the same time teach him appropriate ways of expressing it. Some children initially over eat when they are placed as though they were trying to fill a void in their lives. Others are too depressed or anxious to eat at all.

Foster parent observations during the first few weeks after placement are most helpful, not only in assessing the child's attachment to his parents, but also in assessing the child's interpretation of the placement process and the reasons for placement. Often, when a child comes into care on an emergency basis, he has abruptly lost his parents. His feelings are similar to those that would occur had they been in a terrible accident, and he does not know what will happen next.

Visits soon after placement are necessary to reassure the child that his parents are still alive and do still care about him. This is different from the traditional stance that the child needs an 'adjustment period'. Children in placement need pictures of both parents and siblings.

These visits are apt to tap further into both the child's and parents' strong feelings about separation. It is often much easier for the social workers and for the foster parents when there are fewer contacts between parent and child or if the child does not react to the visits that occur. However, once again, the child cannot deal with these feelings if he cannot express them. The long-term prognosis is worse for children who have few contacts with their parents and minimal reaction to these contacts.

Visits do often make things difficult for foster parents and they may need help in dealing with them. Ner Littner (1971) has written an excellent article on this topic that should be shared with all foster parents. 'Only people cry', a story by Alice Winter (1963) tells of a child's reactions to multiple moves from the child's perspective and is also a helpful article for foster parents to read.

When a child stays in a foster home
While a child is in a foster family, it is very helpful if the family puts together or contributes to a book about that child. This book can

35

include pictures of important events in the child's life in that family and descriptions of how he felt during those events. Examples of things that should be included in such a book are:

- *when the child had particular childhood diseases;*
- *what things he was afraid of;*
- *what toys he liked;*
- *what he did on birthdays and at Christmas;*
- *what trips he took with the foster family;*
- *who important members of the foster family's extended family were;*
- *what cute things the child did;*
- *what his nicknames were;*
- *what he did when he was happy or excited.*

A basic requirement is that the child have a picture of the foster family, their house, and their pets. It is often easiest to retrieve this picture if it is kept in the case file on the family. The book will be something the child can take with him on a future move, whether back to his biological family, to another foster home, or into adoption. It can ease such a transition by preserving the child's continuity with his past.

Exercise 2:
Feelings at the time of moves

Directions: Read the list below of feelings that children may experience at the time of moves. Then, in the lefthand column, list several children in your caseload and on the right, identify the feelings that they may have had about moving. You will probably identify several feelings for each child.

Possible feelings: Anxiety, fear, happiness, anger, sadness, loss, rejection, excitement, jealousy, guilt, resignation, helplessness, relief. You may think of other feelings.

Child	Feelings
1.	
2.	
3.	
4.	

Identifying and overcoming problems

Case example

Richard, a particularly sensitive and perceptive nine-year-old, had spent much of his life in foster care. He was having problems with lying, stealing, getting his work done at school, and getting along with his peers.

During our first interview he asked, off-handedly, 'By the way, do you know what happens to kids who don't get enough loving when they are little?'

I responded, 'Well, I think I know. But I'd like to hear what you think.'

'If kids don't get enough loving when they are three or four or five they become uncontrollable later,' he replied. 'Some foster kids who are eight, nine, and ten can't be controlled by their foster parents.'

I asked 'What do you think can be done about that?'

'I don't know,' he said, 'but I know what you think. You think if they get extra loving later on it will make up for it.'

Introduction

Many children in foster care do not have normal, healthy attachments to their foster parents. The children's attachment problems frequently originate in their birth families. However, the instability of foster home placements and the series of moves that many foster children experience give them further problems in developing trust in others and a sense of age-appropriate autonomy.

The signs and symptoms of attachment problems that one may see in a particular foster child are a result of the way his parents behaved toward him, his environment, and his own particular psychological traits. In general, children who have been severely neglected are the most apt to suffer from a true lack of attachment. Children who have experienced less severe neglect, intermittent physical abuse, or emotional abuse are more likely to exhibit signs of an imbalance in their needs for dependency and their needs for autonomy.

In this section, we outline specific kinds of problems that are frequently exhibited by children who have experienced faulty attachments to their parents. These problems are grouped into three categories: cognitive problems; psychological and behavioural problems; and delays in development. The check list that follows outlines some of the specific problems that may be seen in each of these areas.

After discussing these problems, we consider ways to encourage attachment in the children who are experiencing them. We believe the ability to help build an attachment between a child and his primary caretaker is critical.

Given the potential long-term effects that lack of attachment can have on a child, it is crucial that foster care respond in two ways. First, it should encourage attachment between the children and their present primary caretaker, whomever that may be. Even if the plan for a child in foster care is to return him to his biological family or to move him into an adoptive home, the development of an attachment to his foster parents should be encouraged.

The immediate need is for the child to learn trust. Further delay only makes it more difficult for him. Once a child has experienced one healthy attachment, it becomes easier for him either to transfer this attachment to someone else or to form additional attachments.

Second, it is necessary to make timely permanent plans for children in care. This will limit the number of times children must move and experience the loss of the person to whom they are attached.

Effects of lack of attachment

Lack of attachment and its relationship to psychological and behavioural problems

Bowlby (1970) has noted that unattached children have difficulties relating normally with others. For example, foster and adoptive parents of these children may feel that the children do not have a conscience, are manipulative, or are not genuine in their expression of affection. These parents may say 'I give and I give to this child, and it doesn't seem to matter.'

How do these kinds of symptoms relate to lack of attachment? Remember that a child's first relationship with his primary caretaker sets the stage for his future relationship. In this first relationship the child learns what he can and cannot expect from others. Children who do not experience a healthy give and take in this relationship may not be able to experience it in others.

It is most difficult for the unattached child to grow socially. They have great difficulty learning to build and maintain relationships of any sort. They haven't learned to care for others. Having received little love they have trouble giving it. They continue in their 'babyish' ways, self-centred and acting impulsively. They have difficulty incorporating rules or laws. Their first concern is 'What's in it for me?'

Because the children do not trust others, many of the kinds of behaviour seen in such children are aimed at keeping people at a distance. When one keeps this in mind, it is possible to see similarities in symptoms that would otherwise seem very different. Some of the behaviour patterns children exhibit to keep people at distance are described below.

Observation checklist:
Long-range effects of lack of normal attachment

Psychological or behavioural problems

Conscience development
- May not show normal anxiety following aggressive or cruel behaviour.
- May not show guilt on breaking laws or rules.
- May project blame on others.

Impulse control
- Exhibits poor control; depends upon others to provide external controls on behaviour.
- Exhibits lack of foresight.
- Has a poor attention span.

Self-esteem
- Is unable to get satisfaction from tasks well done.
- Sees self as undeserving.
- Sees self as incapable of change.
- Has difficulty having fun.

Interpersonal interactions
- Lacks trust in others.
- Demands affection but lacks depth in relationships.
- Exhibits hostile dependency.
- Needs to be in control of all situations.
- Has impaired social maturity.

Emotions
- Has trouble recognising own feelings.
- Has difficulty expressing feelings appropriately; especially anger, sadness, and frustration.
- Has difficulty recognising feelings in others.

Cognitive problems

- Has trouble with basic cause and effect.
- Experiences problems with logical thinking.
- Appears to have confused thought processes.
- Has difficulty thinking ahead.
- May have an impaired sense of time.
- Has difficulties with abstract thinking.

Developmental problems

- May have difficulty with auditory processing.
- May have difficulty expressing self well verbally.
- May have gross motor problems.
- May experience delays in fine-motor adaptive skills.
- May experience delays in personal-social development.
- May have inconsistent levels of skills in all of the above areas.

Poor eye contact

In Section 2 on 'The development of attachment between parent and child' we discussed the importance of eye contact to bonding between parent and child. It is not surprising that many children in foster care make little eye contact with others. Many are truly surprised that anyone wants to look at them.

In most abusive families, there is a struggle for control in the family. The parents in these disturbed families are very threatened when the children attempt to gain any control. If a child looks a parent in the eye, the disturbed parent may see that action as a challenge. Abused children tend to be very aware of what is going on around them, however, they tend to check things out by means of sidelong glances rather than direct eye contact.

Withdrawal

Many children with attachment problems withdraw from interactions with others. This withdrawal takes different forms. Some children withdraw physically. Others seem to put up a shield around them; they may be physically near but not close emotionally.

A third type of withdrawal resembles fear. As the parent reaches out to the child, he cringes. If the parent hugs the child, he pulls away or tightens up. All children who withdraw from physical closeness this way have not been abused. Some may have simply learned about the effect their behaviour has on adults. Adults do not want to scare children. Thus, eventually the child learns that cringing, fearful behaviour works to keep adults at a distance.

Chronic anxiety

When a child is confident that his parent will be available when needed, he is less prone to anxiety that is intense or chronic. The most frightening situation for the child is one in which he needs his parent and that parent is not available. This kind of anxiety is greater in children who have been moved without preparation or who have had other major changes in their lives occur abruptly. Children who experience chronic anxiety are also often very possessive and clinging.

Aggressive behaviour

Some children keep adults at a distance by behaving aggressively. If an adult is hit, kicked, scratched, or bitten every time he approaches a child, he is likely to learn to keep his distance. If children have tantrums whenever a demand is placed on them, many parents find it easier to stop making demands. Hyperactive behaviour also keeps adults away. It is difficult to get close to a child who is always on the move and easily distractable.

Case example

Eric is five years old. He has been in foster care for two years. During that time he has been in three different foster homes because he is 'uncontrollable'. Prior to entering foster care he had a history of extreme neglect and moderate abuse.

*In his current foster home Eric has tantrums when he is asked either
to do something or to stop doing something. When he has a tantrum he
kicks at the walls, furniture, or people. One time he threw a toy car at
the television set and broke the screen. Another time he made a big
hole in his bedroom door. During these outbursts he screams, sometimes
for an hour or more. Occasionally he scratches his face or hits himself
on the head as well.*

Indiscriminate affection

Although a normal child may be very talkative and sociable with
strangers, the talk is rarely accompanied by physical overtures. On the
other hand the child who is indiscriminately physically affectionate
may go up, hug a virtual stranger, and say 'I love you'. He, or more
commonly, she, will immediately climb up on the lap of the visitors to
their home and start to hug and kiss them. These interactions frequently
have a seductive quality about them.

If the child behaves this way toward many adults — or virtually all
adults — the child is really saying 'No one is more important to me than
others.' Since attachment means that a few people are more important
than others, indiscriminate affection is a sign of attachment problems.
It is difficult for foster or adoptive parents to feel close to a child who
is acting close to everyone else. In addition, children who are willing to
go with strangers pose real supervision problems for their parents.

Over-competency

Some children with attachment problems seem to be over-competent.
They do not appear to need parents. They frequently insist on doing
everything themselves. These are the pre-schoolers who never seem to
need help with dressing or undressing. Some little girls who are
excessively competent are at age five getting up, making their own beds
and tidying up their rooms without being asked. This may sound like
desirable behaviour, but as anyone who has had a child will recognise,
it is certainly unusual behaviour. When such children do need help,
they may grant the adult permission to help them, as in 'You may tie
my shoes for me.'

Case example

*When we saw Ronald, he was four and a half years old and living with
his father and step-mother. The history revealed that his parents divorced
when he was one and a half years old. He lived with his mother for
about a year after that until she decided she could no longer care for
him financially. She and Ronald travelled several thousand miles by
plane to the town where Ronald's father lived. Ronald was handed over
to his father in a park.*

*Ronald didn't trust his step-mother, and he showed it in several ways.
However, the behaviour she complained most of was his extreme over-
competency. He refused to let her take care of him. For example, if she
tried to help him dress, he would immediately thereafter totally undress*

42

himself and start again. He indicated that he had no need for her. This
over-competency was evident in all aspects of his daily living situation.

Lack of self-awareness

Some abused children seem very aware of their environment but nearly unaware of their own bodies. They may overeat until their stomachs are distended, and they are at the point of vomiting. They may not react to pain and seem unaware of extremes of temperature. Many of these children are bedwetters. It is as if they never learned to pay attention to the signals from their own bodies or to what alleviates their own discomfort.

Such behaviour may develop in children whose parents are unresponsive to them in infancy. Some abusive parents take care of the child when they feel like it, rather than when the child needs it. Thus, the child does not learn to associate certain kinds of discomfort with certain kinds of relief.

Case example

When we first saw John he was six years old and had recently been adopted. He had a history of abuse and neglect and had lived with several families prior to his adoption. He had problems with overeating and with wetting both at night and during the day.

During one post-placement visit we made to the adoptive family, John complained of a stomach ache. He asked his mother if she thought he was hungry. She doubted that he was and suggested that maybe he needed to go to the bathroom. He said 'No', that he didn't think that was the problem.

After John moaned and groaned for several more minutes, his mother said 'John, I want you to go upstairs to the bathroom. If that's not it, O.K., but I want you to try.' John went upstairs and returned with an obvious expression of relief on his face. This six-year-old child had not learned to distinguish between the empty feeling that accompanies hunger for food and the feeling of a full bladder.

Control battles

Both the lack of trust for others that poorly attached children have and the family power struggles that many abused children have witnessed contribute to problems such children have with control issues. Such children have trouble staying within clearly defined limits of behaviour. They appear to be constantly testing. Reasonable requests from parents lead to major confrontations.

Though outwardly these children seem to need to be in control of all situations, they actually feel that they have little control over their lives. This may come from being abused unpredictably, from being moved abruptly, or from experiencing other sudden major life changes.

The two or twenty syndrome

There are certain poorly attached children that appear 'too old for their ages' part of the time and immature at other times. They seem to receive little gratification for acting their chronological age.

Such children try to engage in activities usually preferred by older children. When they play with children their own age, they want to be in charge. They want few restrictions placed on their behaviour. In some ways, they act like an independent, twenty-year-old.

However, if someone sets limits on their behaviour or if they are frustrated, they revert to temper tantrums typical of two-year-olds. Teachers usually describe these children as immature because in a structured school situation their 'babyish' resistance to controls is more evident.

Delayed conscience development

Children with delayed conscience development tend to lie and steal. They may lie about very unimportant things even when there would be no negative consequences for telling the truth. It may also be difficult to tell when such children are lying.

The stealing they do may take the form of 'finding' things frequently at school, of taking money or other things from their family, or of stealing from stores. They often do not show signs of anxiety when they are caught. In fact, they may continue to deny their actions in the face of evidence of their misbehaviour.

Lack of attachment and its relationship to cognitive and developmental problems

Some of the symptoms exhibited by children who have had poor attachments are the same symptoms that are exhibited by children with what is called 'minimal brain dysfunction'. Children with minimal brain dysfunction may be hyperactive, easily distractable, impulsive, subject to extremes of emotions and have learning disabilities. They may, in other words, be children who seem to have a very short attention span, or who seem to 'always act before they think'.

They may also overreact to what is going on around them. For example, if a child gently brushes by a hyperactive child, the hyperactive child may perceive this as an open invitation to fight. Such children may have a very low tolerance for frustration. They may have difficulty moving from one task to another if they view the first task as incomplete

A higher proportion of the children who come into care have minimal brain dysfunction than one would expect based on the proportion of children who have this problem in the population as a whole. One can speculate about whether these children were born with certain organic problems that made it difficult for them to form attachments, or whether the lack of attachment between the child and his parent precipitated certain organic problems.

There is increasing evidence of a strong genetic component in minimal brain dysfunction. Interestingly, it is possible that many of the parents of children in care experience minimal brain dysfunction themselves.

What kind of adults do children with minimal brain dysfunction become? There have been some recent studies that indicate that a high

44

percentage of these individuals continue to have difficulties in adult life although hyperactivity *per se* usually diminishes during adolescent years. Many such individuals continue to be rigid in their thinking and expectations. They may remain emotionally unstable and unable to tolerate frustration. In addition, they may have a variety of other problems as a result of growing up in a school system that was not equipped to meet their needs. The literature affirms that many juvenile delinquents have a history of school problems and of learning disabilities.

Many of the parents of the children who come into care have problems like those outlined above. Thus, if we speculate that there is a higher incidence of minimal brain dysfunction among the parents of these children than in the population as a whole, from a genetic viewpoint, we would also expect to see a higher incidence of it in children of this population.

However, in addition to genetic determinants of these problems, they seem to be affected by parent-child attachments as well. This should not be unexpected if we consider several well known facts. Prior to birth the foetus possesses its full complement of neurons. If these neurons are damaged there will be virtually no regeneration. Thus, before the infant is born, his maximum intellectual potential is set. However, during the latter months of pregnancy and during infancy and early childhood, the task at hand is to get the neurons organised into patterns of responsiveness.

According to Gesell (1946) during the first year of life the infant must learn how to learn. People learn new things throughout their lives, but they learn them in an established way. As the child matures, his perceptions become more discerning and he notices things he didn't previously notice. He incorporates these perceptions into his basic fund of knowledge.

It is through his relationship with his mother in his first year of life that the child learns how to learn. The reciprocity in this relationship helps the child sort out his perceptions of the world and teaches him what these perceptions mean. At birth, an infant does not recognise objects in his environment or specific internal states of being. He does not know, for example, that a certain state of discomfort that we call 'hunger' is relieved by the intake of food. However, if his mother consistently identifies that discomfort with an empty stomach, the child learns to perceive that feeling as hunger for food. It is through this relationship with his primary caretaker that the child first learns cause and effect and thus learns how to learn.

Thus we could speculate that minimal brain dysfunction has two basic causes: it may occur for genetically determined structural or biochemical reasons. This kind of problem would not be affected by the adequacy and appropriateness of the mothering the child receives. It may occur in the child who has not experienced the mothering necessary to get a reasonably organised nervous system.

Practically speaking, by the time the child is old enough so that the nature of his perceptual problems can be identified, determining their underlying cause does not matter much. The important thing then is

45

helping the child compensate for his perceptual deficits and providing stimulation to encourage further growth.

Children with minimal brain dysfunction frequently fail to perceive their surroundings accurately. Their misperceptions form a base from which they learn and incorporate new experiences. To help such a child those around him must carefully observe the child and identify his misperceptions. Having done this, it is possible to correct the misperceptions and improve the way the child learns.

Children with minimal brain dysfunction find it more difficult than other children to handle changes in their environment and separation from those to whom they are attached. They are more prone to anxiety than other children. Their behaviour makes it difficult for their parents or foster parents to deal with them in a way that encourages bonding. This kind of response from the parents makes the child even more anxious, and what appears to be a never ending negative cycle is created.

Exercise 3:
Identifying signs of lack of attachment — instructions

Purpose:
*To help you learn to identify signs of lack of attachment or
faulty attachment.*

How to do it:
1. *Read Roberta's case history on the next page.*

2. *Using the worksheet, list comments and/or observations from
the case record that you feel indicate Roberta's lack of
attachment or faulty attachment.*

3. *After working on your list, look at page 49 where a sample
analysis of the case appears and compare your worksheet
with the sample.*

Roberta, who is now eight and a half years old, was abandoned by her birth mother when she was one year old. At that time, she was functioning at a six to eight month old developmental level. During the following year in foster care she closed most of the gaps between her chronological age and her developmental age. She was placed for adoption at age two.

The adoption disrupted a year and a half ago because 'Roberta never really got close' to the adoptive parents. She has lived in three foster homes since then. Her pattern in foster care has been to be superficially compliant but after several months the foster parents describe her as being 'sneaky' and 'there is just something about her'.

In her present foster home the history reveals that she sneaks food and hides it in her room. This behaviour tends to make her foster mother very angry. She occasionally sleepwalks and cries out in her sleep. She is enuretic several times a week. She loves to help her foster mother in the kitchen but 'forgets' her routine chores such as tidying up her room and stripping her bed when it is wet.

Roberta has difficulty getting along with her foster siblings. She takes the teen-aged daughter's make-up and then denies taking it. When she plays games with the other pre-adolescents, she always disrupts the game if she sees that she is not going to win. Roberta becomes totally enraged by events that lead to irritation or annoyance in most children.

At school she does well in reading, but hates maths. She does complete her papers, but they are frequently so messy that they are unreadable. She is frequently out of her seat without permission, she talks out in class and is always either the first or the last in line.

The teacher reports that Roberta has difficulty getting along with peers. She has just started in the third form but she prefers to play with the first formers at recess. In the foster home, too, she plays best with a younger foster sibling whom she tries to boss.

The teacher comments that Roberta 'just seems to need more love'. Roberta frequently tells her how the foster parents prefer the other children to her. In fact the teacher bought her a pair of sandals after Roberta had complained that everyone else had got new sandals except her. Roberta clings to her teacher and wants to give her hugs and kisses every morning when she comes to school. Roberta behaves in a similar fashion with her social worker when she comes to the home.

When introduced to a female psychologist Roberta's first comment was 'Oh, I hope you are my new social worker: I just love to get new social workers'. When asked how she felt about mothers, her comment was 'Well, I don't like mothers too well. They always know what you are doing'.

48

Exercise 3:
Identifying signs of lack of attachment — sample response

1. 'Roberta never really got close' (adoptive parents).

2. 'Sneaky' 'something about her' (foster parents).

3. Might terrors

4. Enuretic (lack of self-awareness?)

5. Steals, doesn't do chores, lies (conscience development)

6. Over-reacts (i.e, when losing games)

7. Can't get along with kids her own age

8. Bossy with younger kids (over-competent?)

9. 'Indiscriminate affection' (i.e, teachers and Social workers)

10. Not in touch with feelings (i.e,' just love to get a new social worker!')

11. Messy papers? (fine motor developmental delay or lack of self esteem or doesn't want to mind.)

12.

Promoting attachment in older children

When children have not experienced healthy attachments and are beyond infancy, how can someone help make up for it? We address this question briefly in the text and charts that follow.

In Section 2 on 'The development of attachment between parent and child' we described two cycles related to bonding in infants. One of these cycles was called the 'arousal-relaxation cycle' and the other patterns of interactions between parent and child that result in bonding. They are diagrammed below. These cycles can be adapted to older children as well.

The arousal-relaxation cycle

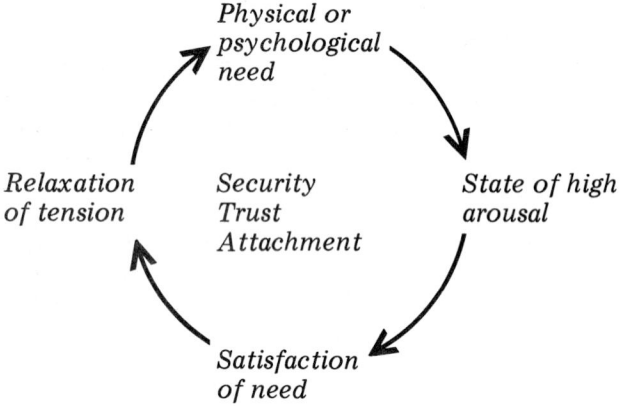

Physical or psychological need

State of high arousal

Satisfaction of need

Relaxation of tension

Security Trust Attachment

The cycle of positive interactions

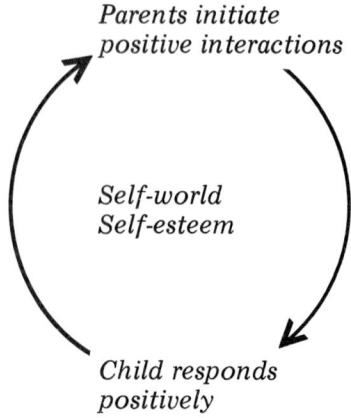

Parents initiate positive interactions

Self-world Self-esteem

Child responds positively

In analysing interactions that occur between an older child and a parent in terms of the arousal-relaxation cycle, it is important to be aware of several things. First, the child's needs that initiate the cycle may be either physical or psychological. The important thing is that these needs create intense feelings or states of high arousal in the child. The intense feelings may be negative, such as anxiety, fear, anger, rage, or sadness or positive, such as joy or excitement. The parent's role with these children might be not so much to satisfy the need themselves but just to be with the child and encourage his expression of feelings until the body tension that accompanies his intense feelings relaxes. At this time of relaxation the child is most open to bonding.

For example, when a child gets extremely frustrated and has a temper tantrum, at the end of that tantrum he relaxes and is very open to bonding. When a child is ill and faces a trip to the doctor, he is likely to be highly aroused. A parent who stays with the child through any painful proceedings and allows the child to express his feelings encourages bonding.

Children in care are generally highly aroused at the time of moves. Social workers or new parents who allow and encourage the child to express his feelings are in reality encouraging bonding as well.

The positive interactions cycle works the same way for children who are beyond infancy as it does in infancy. Parents initiate positive things with the child, the child responds positively, and both parties are likely to continue. It is easiest for parents to begin initiating positive interactions with a child when he first moves in. This makes it less likely that parent and child will have to work to correct a cycle of negative interactions begetting negative interactions.

The other kind of behaviour that families can get involved in to promote attachment is 'claiming behaviour'. Claiming behaviour was first discussed in Section 2 as well.

Social workers need to think of as many ways as possible to help families use these cycles to build attachment with children. The checklist that follows suggests some ways for families to get these positive patterns going.

Remember, both shared laughter and shared tears are powerful bonding tools.

51

Checklist:
Ways to encourage attachment

Responding to the arousal/relaxation cycle

Responding to the arousal/relaxation cycle

- *Using the child's tantrums to encourage attachment.*
- *Responding to the child when he is physically ill.*
- *Accompanying the child to doctor and dentist appointments.*
- *Helping the child express and cope with feelings of anger and frustration.*
- *Sharing the child's extreme excitement over his achievements.*
- *Helping the child cope with feelings about moving.*
- *Helping the child cope with ambivalent feelings about his birth family.*
- *Helping the child learn more about his past.*
- *Responding to a child who is hurt or injured.*
- *Educating the child about sexual issues.*
  others:

Initiating positive interactions

- *Making affectionate overtures: hugs, kisses, physical closeness.*
- *Reading to the child.*
- *Sharing the child's Life Book.*
- *Playing games.*
- *Going shopping together for clothes/toys for child.*
- *Going on special outings: circus, plays, or the like.*
- *Supporting the child's outside activities by providing transport or being a group leader,*
- *Helping the child with homework when he or she needs it.*
- *Teaching the child to cook or bake.*
- *Saying 'I love you'.*
- *Teaching the child about extended family members through pictures and talk.*
- *Helping the child understand the family 'jokes' or sayings.*
- *Teaching the child to participate in family activities such as bowling, camping, or ski-ing.*
- *Helping the child meet expectations of the other parent. others:*

52

Checklist:
Ways to encourage attachment

Responding to the arousal/relaxation cycle

Claiming behaviour

- *Encouraging the child to practise calling parents 'mum' and 'dad'.*
- *Adding a middle name to incorporate a name of family significance.*
- *Hanging pictures of child on wall.*
- *Involving the child in family reunions and similar activities.*
- *Involving the child in grand-parent visits.*
- *Including the child in family rituals.*
- *Holding religious ceremonies or other ceremonies that incor-porate the child into the family.*
- *Buying new clothes for the child as a way of becoming acquainted with child's size; colour prefer-ences; style preferences, and the like.*
- *Making statements such as 'in our family do it this way' in supportive fashion.*
- *Sending out announcements of adoption.*
  others:

53

Exercise 4:
Encouraging attachment — instructions

Purpose:
To help you practise defining ways to encourage attachment.

How to do it:
1 *Read Sharon's case history on the next page.*

2 *Using the worksheet for this exercise, list as many ways as you can think of that the family might use in helping Sharon develop attachment to them.*

3 *After working on your list, look at the sample that one worker developed.*

4 *Now, pick a child in your caseload who has moved recently. First, summarise the case. Then, develop the same type of list for your own case as you did for Sharon.*

Sharon is an eight-year-old girl who is being placed for adoption in a family with three older boys. Past history reveals that Sharon experienced considerable emotional and physical deprivation, rejection, and physical abuse from her birth parents. She has had seven moves since she first entered care at age three.

Sharon has many fears including fear of the dark and fear of new situations. She is prone to nightmares. There is a history of both day-time and night-time wetting. She is a very demanding child who verbally pressures and manipulates adults. She gets little pleasure from being a child and prefers to 'pretend' that she is an adolescent going out on dates. She is very seductive in her relationships with males.

Sharon has many gaps in her basic fund of knowledge; she exhibits problems with logical thinking and basic cause and effect. Sharon has many problems with lying; she tends to 'forget' what she chooses not to hear. Her lying extends even to saying 'that is my favourite food' when in reality it is a food she dislikes. Other times her lying is aimed at keeping herself out of trouble.

She has marked difficulties with peer relationships. She does well in the self-help skills. She likes to help with household tasks. In school, she is reading above her age level but has some difficulty with maths. She shows appropriate responses and is an attractive girl who is quite outgoing. Her self-esteem is poor as indicated by comments such as 'something is wrong with me', when she makes an error. She is able to talk about feelings and can tell of many ways that she and her present foster parents have fun together.

Exercise 4:
Encouraging attachment — sample response

Arousal relaxation cycle	Positive interaction cycle
1. parents could sit with Sharon, after her awaking from nightmares	1. Doing household tasks with Sharon.
2. Help Sharon talk about her fears	2. Looking at life book
3. Arrange a visit with previous foster parents	3. Help Sharon with Maths homework
4. Help Sharon talk about past foster families.	4. Organise outings for Sharon and her new brother
5. Develop a life book	5. Mother give Sharon hugs, kisses, physical closeness,
	6. Give Sharon good choices.
6. Confront Sharon about lies or stealing and assist her in correcting the situation and support her afterwards	7. Get Sharon to join a group (i.e, brownies).
	8. Explain sex with Sharon

Claiming behaviour

1. Get a family portrait including Sharon.	3. Buy new clothes for Sharon (will also positively reinforce her attractiveness).
2. Have a family get-together to introduce Sharon	4. Sharon is to practice calling her new parents 'mum and Dad'.

Encouraging attachment — worksheet 2

Your own case

Case summary:
Arousal/relaxation cycle
Positive interaction cycle
Claiming behaviour

Case planning for attachment

Directions:
Which children in your caseload did you think of as you read through this workbook? Identify three or four who have attachment/separation problems and outline a specific plan for each child to either encourage attachment, transfer attachment, or help child and family deal with separation issues.

Child
Concerns
Plan

Exercise 5:
Case planning for attachment

Child

Concerns

Plan

References

Ainsworth, M.D. and Boston, M., 'Psychodiagnostic Assessments of a Child after Prolonged Separation in Early Childhood', *Brit. J. Med. Psychol.*, 25: 169-201, 1952.

Bowlby, J., 'Attachment and Loss', Vol 1, *Attachment*, New York: Basic Books, 1970.

Delacato, Carl H., *The Ultimate Stranger*, New York: Doubleday & Co. Inc., 1974.

Desmond, M.M., Rudolph, A.J. and Phitaksphraiwan, P., 'The Transitional Care Nursery: A Mechanism of a Preventative Medicine', *Pediatric Clinics of North America*, 13: 651-668, 1966.

Fraiberg, Selma, *Every Child's Birthright: In Defense of Mothering*, New York: Basic Books, 1977.

Gessell, Arnold and Ilg, Frances, *The First Five Years of Life: A Guide to the Study of the Pre-School Child*, New York: Harper and Row, 1946.

Kennell, J., Voos, D. and Klaus, M., 'Parent-Infant Bonding' in Helfer, R. and Kempe, C.H. (eds.), *Child Abuse and Neglect*, Cambridge, Mass: Ballinger Publishing Co., 1976.

Littner, Ner, 'The Importance of the Natural Parents to the Child in Placement', *Child Welfare*, Vol LIV, 54, March, 1975.

Lorenz, Konrad, *On Aggression*, New York: Harcourt, Brace Co., 1966.

Moss, H.A. and Robson, J.S., 'Maternal Influences in Early Social Visual Behavior', *Child Development*, 39: 401-403, 1968.

Spitz, R., *The First Year of Life*, New York: International Universities Press, 1965.

Winter, Alice, 'Only People Cry', *Woman's Day Magazine*, September, 1963.

Wolff, P.H., *The Causes, Controls and Organization of Behavior in the Neonate*, New York: International Universities Press, 1966.

Yarrow, L.J., 'Research in Dimensions of Early Maternal Care', *Merrill-Palmer Quarterly*, 9: 101-14, 1965.

Printed by
Witley Press Ltd, Norfolk

Designed by
Ivor Kamlish FSIAD & Associates